21.26

Water

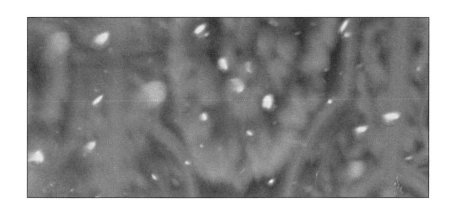

by Henry Pluckrose

Gareth Stevens Publishing
A WORLD ALMANAC EDUCATION GROUP COMPANY

Please visit our web site at: **www.garethstevens.com**
For a free color catalog describing Gareth Stevens' list of high-quality books
and multimedia programs, call 1-800-542-2595 (USA) or 1-800-461-9120 (Canada).
Gareth Stevens Publishing's Fax: (414) 332-3567.

Library of Congress Cataloging-in-Publication Data

Pluckrose, Henry Arthur.
    Water / by Henry Pluckrose. — North American ed.
        p. cm. — (Let's explore)
    Includes bibliographical references and index.
    ISBN 0-8368-2968-9 (lib. bdg.)
    1. Water—Juvenile literature. I. Title.
    GB662.3.P68   2001
    553.7—dc21   2001031108

This North American edition first published in 2001 by
Gareth Stevens Publishing
A World Almanac Education Group Company
330 West Olive Street, Suite 100
Milwaukee, WI 53212 USA

This U.S. edition © 2001 by Gareth Stevens, Inc. Original edition © 2000 by Franklin Watts.
First published in 2000 by Franklin Watts, 96 Leonard Street, London, EC2A 4XD, United
Kingdom. Additional end matter © 2001 by Gareth Stevens, Inc.

Series editor: Louise John
Series designer: Jason Anscomb
Gareth Stevens editor: Monica Rausch
Gareth Stevens designer: Katherine A. Kroll

Picture credits: Bruce Coleman Collection pp. 13 (Francisco J. Erize), 20 (Dr. Scott Nielsen);
Robert Harding p. 6 (Raj Kamal); Images Colour Library pp. 9, 11, 19, 21; Ray Moller
Photography p. 15; Steve Shott Photography p. 16; Still Pictures pp. 4 (Gunter Ziesler),
26 (Martin Harvey), 24 (John Isaac), 28 (KITTPREMPOOL-UNEP), 31 (F. Polking); Tony Stone
Images p. 23 and title page (George Kamper).

Printed in the United States of America

1 2 3 4 5 6 7 8 9 05 04 03 02 01

Contents

These heavy, dark clouds are made of tiny drops of water. Sometimes the small drops of water in clouds join together to make larger and larger drops. When the drops become too large and too heavy for the air to hold, they fall as rain.

Some of the rain soaks into the ground. Some of it falls into streams, rivers, and lakes. Some even splashes on your head!

The Sun often shines after it rains. The Sun's heat warms the water on the ground and in lakes and rivers. The warm water evaporates, or turns into a gas called water vapor. This vapor rises and cools. When it cools, it turns back into tiny water drops. The drops form new clouds. Soon they will fall again as rain.

Much of the water on Earth is liquid. Liquid water in rivers and streams flows downhill into lakes, seas, and oceans.

When water gets very cold, it freezes, or turns into ice. The North Pole and the South Pole are so cold they are covered with ice all year round.

When water gets very hot, it boils and turns into vapor. The steam coming out of this kettle is water that is evaporating, or turning into vapor.

Some materials dissolve, or mix completely, in water or other liquids. When you stir sugar into water, the grains of sugar disappear. They have dissolved in water.

Some objects float on water, including cruise ships, fishing boats, sailboats, canoes, and even leaves and twigs.

Many animals, such as ducks,
live in or near water.

Ducks use their webbed feet like paddles to help them swim.

People swim, too. We also play many sports in or on water. We can ski, surf, or dive, but we must be very careful around water. Water, especially deep water, can be dangerous.

Water is also good for us. We need to drink water every day to stay alive and healthy.

Plants and animals also need water to live. For all living things, water can be even more important than food.

Some parts of the world do not have enough water. Crops cannot grow and animals will die without water. Without crops and animals, it is difficult for people to find food to eat.

We all need water to live, so we must take care of the water around us. We should try to keep our lakes and rivers clean. We must not waste our precious water.

Index

More Books to Read

Floating and Sinking. Start-Up Science (series).
   Jack Challoner (Raintree/Steck-Vaughn)
The Magic School Bus: At the Waterworks.
   Joanna Cole (Scholastic Trade)
Water: Simple Experiments for Young Scientists.
   Larry White (Millbrook Press)